AF323730

SUPER-CHARGED!

BAJA CARS

BY

T. J. Andersen

PUBLISHED BY

CRESTWOOD HOUSE

Mankato, MN, U.S.A.

CIP

LIBRARY OF CONGRESS CATALOGING IN PUBLICATION DATA

Andersen, T.J.
  Baja cars

  (Super-Charged!)
  Includes index.
  SUMMARY: Describes the history, course, and vehicles of off-road racing with emphasis of the Baja 1000, the longest of the off-road races.
  1. All terrain vehicle racing — Mexico — Baja California — Juvenile literature.   (1. All terrain vehicle racing — Mexico — Baja California.   2. All terrain vehicles.)   I. Title.
GV1037.A53   1988   796.7'2'097223 — dc19   87-29022
ISBN 0-89686-357-3

International Standard Book Number:	Library of Congress Catalog Card Number:
0-89686-357-3	87-29022

CREDITS

Cover: Globe Photos, Inc. : (D. Jones)
FPG International: (Robert Reiff) 14-15
Third Coast Stock Source: (Buck Miller) 21
Rob Gage Photography: 32-33
Centerline Photography: 4-5, 16, 18-19, 28, 29, 30, 31, 34, 35, 42
Globe Photos, Inc.: (Douglas Jones) 7, 13, 23, 24, 43
Focus West: (E. S. Cryer) 10-11; (Robert Brown) 12, 45; (Dave Black) 17;
  (D. Mazzapica) 40, 41; (Todd Friedman) 36-37

Acknowledgements to Steve Kassanyi, Race Director, SCORE International

Produced by Carnival Enterprises.

Box 3427, Mankato, MN, U.S.A. 56002

TABLE OF CONTENTS

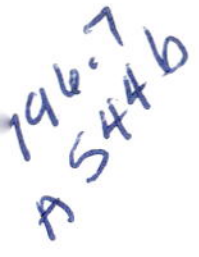

Introduction 4
Beginnings 8
Modern Off-Road Racing .9
Racing Classes and Divisions 13
Special Equipment 16
Safety 20
Off-Road Champions 21
The Racing Team 24
Sponsors 25
Baja 1000 26
Other Major Races 36
Pre-Running 39
The Future 39
Baja Car Divisions 41
For More Information 46
Glossary/Index 47–48

The rough and rugged race course challenges all vehicles that enter the Baja 1000.

INTRODUCTION

It's a perfect morning in Ensenada, a Mexican town not too far south of San Diego, California. The temperature is in the 80's and the sky is a clear blue.

You're sitting behind the wheel of a four-wheel-drive Ford Bronco at the starting line of off-road racing's biggest event, the Baja 1000. With you is another member of your racing team. Two more team members are waiting at a checkpoint approximately

300 miles (482 kilometers) away to relieve you.

Sixty-three participants riding motorcycles, three-wheel all-terrain vehicles, quads, and Odysseys have already started the race. They've been given a one-hour start before you and the rest of the four-wheel vehicles get going. The green flag drops. You're on your way!

Ahead of you are anywhere from 18 to 42 hours of winding dirt roads, sticky swamp land, forest-covered mountains, flat dry lake beds, and sandy shoreline. You'll be criss-crossing the spiny center of the Baja California peninsula all the way from Ensenada down to La Paz. If you follow the route correctly, you will cover 1,013 miles (1,630 kilometers). Many drivers get lost several times and add hundreds of miles to their route.

During your time at the wheel, you'll be bounced around like a steel ball in a pinball machine. You'll pass drivers digging their four-wheel drive vehicles out of the mud. Just as you're congratulating yourself on avoiding their fate, you'll grind to a halt in an even bigger mudhole.

If you and the other member of your team are lucky, some spectators — or perhaps a Mexican farmer or two — will be nearby. You'll convince them to help dig you out of the mud, and an hour later, you'll be back on track. You'll try to gain time across a rocky stretch.

But then you hear a flopping sound, and you feel

Sometimes Baja drivers need a little help from spectators.

your Bronco lurching. It's not hard to recognize the signs of a flat tire. Fortunately, you're just a few miles from a service pit. You decide to limp there on your bad tire because your team members will be waiting for you. They can change the tire faster than you could.

There goes a Baja Bug around you . . . and a motorcycle . . . and a Nissan 4x4. What are you *doing* in this race? You're pitting yourself and your machine against the land, your competitors, and sometimes, against yourself. You're having a great time!

BEGINNINGS

Car and motorcycle enthusiasts have been racing pickups, cars, and motorcycles across open land for a long time. Not until some of them began riding down Mexico's Baja California peninsula, though, did off-road racing begin to emerge as a true sport.

The beginning of the Baja race can be traced to two friends named Dave Ekins and Bill Robertson, Jr. They made the trip from Tijuana to La Paz on motorcycles in 1962. Their course was nearly 1,000 miles (1,609 kilometers) of rough land, and they claimed a record time of 39 hours and 54 minutes. Four years later, Ekins and three other riders took the same route and beat the original time by just five minutes.

In 1967, Bruce Meyers and Ted Mangels charted a new course down the Baja in a Meyers Manx, a modified Volkswagen with a cut-down fiberglass body. Meyers had designed this ultimate dune buggy after seeing old cars with big tires and cut-down bodies tearing across the California beach. Shortly after the Meyers/Mangels tour, drivers in other kinds of vehicles began to follow their route down the peninsula.

Soon an organization, the National Off-Road Racing Association (NORRA), was formed. NORRA's first major racing event was held in October 1967. Called the Mexican 1000, this 950-mile (1,528-kilometer) race was later renamed the Baja 1000.

MODERN OFF-ROAD RACING

There weren't many rules in that first Mexican 1000. Everyone was in the same class, whether on two or four wheels, and there were only five checkpoints along the 950-mile (1,528-kilometer) course. Through 1972, NORRA continued to hold the Baja 1000 every fall and the Baja 500 in the spring. The Baja Internacional, sometimes call the Baja 500, is a 500-mile (804-kilometer) course that

Off-road races are just as much fun as the Baja 1000.

begins and ends in Ensenada.

In 1973 the Mexican government took over the promotion of the Baja races from NORRA. Then in

10

1974, the government asked SCORE International, a newly formed organization, to produce the two racing events. SCORE was established by Mickey

Thompson, a well-known drag racer who had been bitten by the off-road racing bug and wanted to promote it as a spectator sport.

Thompson realized that not many people could see the Baja races because of the great distances they covered, so he organized a short-course race at Riverside, California. Despite some major obstacles, that first event was successful. Today it has grown into an annual event known as the SCORE Off-Road World Championship.

Even production vehicles can enter a Baja race.

Even though it looks funny, this vehicle is tough enough for any off-road race.

Under Mickey Thompson's leadership, SCORE established a well-defined system of racing classes and wrote a rule book. The organization provides agreed-upon standards of racing safety and excellence. Together with another organization, the High Desert Racing Association (HDRA), SCORE organizes and manages eight major events each year.

RACING CLASSES AND DIVISIONS

Almost anyone who wants to can compete in off-road racing. There are categories for first-time

A Baja car's suspension system must be in top condition.

competitors as well as seasoned racers, for production vehicles (cars or trucks built at assembly plants in Detroit or elsewhere) as well as vehicles built especially for off-road races.

Most races are open to two-wheel, three-wheel, and four-wheel vehicles. For four-wheel vehicles alone, there are 16 different classes, divided into three divisions: the Buggy Division, the Heavy Metal

Division, and the Mini Metal Division.

Every year, one competitor in each of these 16 classes becomes the class overall champion. The championship is awarded on the basis of points scored in each of the eight major races organized by SCORE and HDRA. In addition, the class champion who has the highest number of points in each division becomes the division champion.

A spare tire is a must for Baja cars.

SPECIAL EQUIPMENT

Vehicles take a lot of punishment when they are raced off-road. Most vehicles have been modified to withstand the rough conditions they encounter.

The suspension system connects the frame, or chassis of a vehicle, to the axle and wheels. The body of the vehicle and the motor rest on the chassis. With every rock and rut the wheels hit, the suspension system must move to absorb the bump, so that the

16

Mesh cages protect Baja drivers.

rest of the vehicle isn't affected. In off-road race vehicles, many suspension parts are reinforced or replaced with more rugged pieces. Extra shocks are usually added on all four corners.

Off-road racing puts a huge amount of stress on parts of the steering linkage and drivetrain systems. The drivetrain supplies the power from the engine to the wheels. These parts, too, must be reinforced.

The tires that come as standard equipment on a new vehicle are generally meant for pavement

Because the Baja race doesn't end at night, drivers use foglights and spotlights to drive in the dark.

BFGoodrich

driving, not off-road racing. Tires perform differently on different surfaces, such as sand, mud, water, and rocks. Yet the off-road vehicle may have to cover all of these surfaces in one race! There are tires for each of these conditions; in addition, there are all-purpose tires that work pretty well in all conditions. Racing vehicles usually carry two spare tires bolted in place so they don't do any damage as the vehicle bounces over rough terrain.

Many specially built off-road vehicles have mesh cages over the windows to protect them from stones and rocks thrown up by other vehicles. Depending on the kind of vehicle, other modifications for racing include foglights and spotlights, a front brush guard, a roll bar or full roll cage, and an extra fuel tank.

SAFETY

There are certain safety precautions for all race vehicles. All drivers and passengers must wear five-point harnesses. Like seat belts, these consist of two three-inch lap belts, two shoulder straps, and one strap running down to the floor. Drivers and passengers must also wear helmets and fire-retardant driving suits.

Vehicles must be equipped with fire extinguishers and first aid kits. They are also required to have side nets to keep the occupants' arms inside the vehicle.

OFF-ROAD CHAMPIONS

Off-road racing is still a young sport, and some of its stars have been around from the beginning. Many people who compete in races are also involved in off-roading in other ways. Some are mechanics, car designers, or kit car manufacturers. Others own body shops or parts stores.

Walker Evans has been the Class 8 champion several different years. He discovered off-road racing

Shoulder straps and fire-retardant suits are a must for all Baja drivers.

in 1970, and during the mid-1970's he drove a Dodge pickup. In 1977 he started his own off-road racing shop, Walker Evans Enterprises, in Riverside, California. The shop builds a limited number of vehicles each year, including the one Evans now drives, a Dodge Ram D50 truck.

The "King of Class 3," Don Adams, is a real estate broker who lives with his family in the Colorado mountains. Don's racing career began in the '60's, when he raced sports cars on the track. He began off-road racing in 1971 and over the years has competed in Class 3, Class 4, and Class 2 races. In 1985, Don began driving the new Jeep Cherokee.

Class 4 champion Rod Hall drove in the first Baja 1000 in 1967 and finished in seventh place overall. Since then, he has had eight wins in the Baja 1000 and dozens of wins in other races, including some in Africa and Australia. Rod and his family live in Reno, Nevada, where they own and operate Rod Hall International, a company that modifies Dodge pickup trucks. Rod also writes a syndicated newspaper column with advice for off-roaders.

Other well-known racers who consistently finish in front are Manny Esquerra, Bobby Ferro, Glenn Harris, Mark McMillin, Ivan Stewart, Roger Mears, and Johnny Johnson.

The pit crew and drivers double-check all equipment before the start of a race.

GASOLINA
Espinoza
NEVADA ROCK & SAND
READY MIX
BELL S. JOB CONCRETE
DRIVERS
DARRELL THORNTON
GARY STEWART
BELL
172

The chase crew is prepared to fix big and small problems.

THE RACING TEAM

None of these men has gotten to the championship level alone. Most have competed in cars built by other racing teams or have driven factory-sponsored vehicles. Even those competitors who build their own cars need other people for specialized work.

Racers are usually part of a driving team of two or more people. For years, Rod Hall's co-driver has been Jim Fricker; Don Adams now races with Larry Olson. Walker Evans prefers to go solo and drive the entire race by himself. But Evans, like everyone else, is backed by a chase crew and a pit crew.

24

The chase crew is the group of people that "chases" the racer in another vehicle, not off-road but on the pavement. The chase crew is prepared to provide emergency help between the regular pit stops. The chase crew meets the race vehicle at pre-arranged spots along the route. Normally, the race vehicle and the chase vehicle are in radio contact. If there's trouble, such as a flat tire, the chase crew is alerted and will be prepared to change it. The personnel in the chase crew can range from uniformed factory teams to an assortment of friends and family!

Along the route at regular intervals are well-equipped pits where racers stop for gas, tire changes, and other routine work. Some pit crews, such as the B.F. Goodrich pit, serve more than one racing team and will help out other teams.

Besides being in contact with chase crews and pit crews by phone or radio, some driving teams wear wired helmets so they can talk to each other — passenger and driver — over the roar of the engine.

SPONSORS

It's not unusual for a racing team to have sponsors. All of the well-known racers, and even some of the newcomers, have a sponsor to help offset the high cost of off-road racing. Although off-road race vehicles are not nearly as expensive as other kinds of race cars, they take a severe beating and their parts need frequent replacing.

When a company sponsors a racing team, its name is usually displayed somewhere on the racing vehicle. That gives the company publicity and lets people know that that company's product is being used on that vehicle. If the vehicle is a winner, so is the product.

Some of the sponsoring companies are manufacturers of auto parts or accessories, such as tires, foglights, or shock absorbers. Others are car and truck manufacturers, such as Toyota, Chrysler, Ford, and Nissan.

In return for their financial support, manufacturers get to see their products tested under rugged conditions. Factory-supported vehicles become rolling laboratories as racers try out tires, suspension components, and drivetrain components. This way, manufacturers can continue to improve the quality of their cars to meet the off-road racer's needs.

BAJA 1000

The Baja 1000 is the longest of the important off-road races. Although the exact route can vary from year to year, the race usually begins in Ensenada and ends in La Paz, on the tip of the Baja California peninsula. The race route is marked with orange flags.

Drivers show-off their Baja vehicles before the race.

Competitors arrive in Ensenada the day before the race for the technical inspection. Teams push their vehicles through the main street of Ensenada, where onlookers have a chance to see the vehicles in mint condition, before they set off.

Many challenges lie ahead for the racers in the Baja 1000.

The race usually begins at about dawn. The motorcycles and three-wheel vehicles are given an hour's head start so they can be safely on their way before the four-wheel vehicles start. Then the cars and trucks are flagged off one by one, and their starting times are recorded.

The terrain varies quite a bit. In some cases, the route follows dirt roads used by Mexican farmers to

A dusty road can't stop this Baja truck.

haul produce into the village, and drivers are likely to meet one or more old trucks chugging along on the road. Competitors must also watch out for animals—anything from cows and horses to chickens and dogs—that wander unexpectedly across the dirt road.

In other cases, the route follows a trail even less used—and for good reason! The difference between getting bogged down in mud and silt and avoiding it can be just a few feet in either direction. Drivers have to know when to speed up and force their way through the mud and when to go around it. Other hazards include narrow ledges of rock, steep grades, and sudden turns. The route goes through small towns and villages with names like Santa Ines, El Arco, San Ignacio, and El Tomate.

Not everyone who enters the Baja 1000 finishes the race. Many competitors get hopelessly stuck or

Baja drivers face all types of obstacles.

The dreaded mud-hole!

The Baja race course cuts right through the desert.

their vehicles break down somewhere on the route. Only about 60 percent of the entries who started in the 1986 Baja 1000 finished within the 42-hour time limit. The fastest overall time for a car was logged by Mark McMillin and Ralph Paxton (Class 1) at just

The Baja 1000 winners celebrate their victory.

over 18 hours, 26 minutes.

Those who do manage to finish are greeted by crowds of spectators and well-wishers at the Gran Baja Hotel in La Paz. Just finishing this incredibly difficult event is cause for celebration!

OTHER MAJOR RACES

At about 1,000 miles (1,609 kilometers) long, the Baja 1000 is the longest of the eight races that count toward the SCORE-HDRA championship totals (the number in the name of each race indicates its approximate length). Usually scheduled in early November, the Baja 1000 is the last race on the yearly calendar. A ninth major event, the SCORE Off-Road World Championship, held in the Riverside

Baja cars compete in track races, too.

International Raceway, is not included as part of these totals.

The racing year begins with the SCORE Parker 400, scheduled in late January or early February. The Parker 400 starts in the California desert, runs on both sides of the Colorado River, and finishes in Parker, Arizona. Although much of the route is straight, ruts alternate with beds of silt on a narrow course.

The Gold Coast 300, held in March, and the Mint

400, held in May, are both organized by HDRA and are held in Las Vegas. Both races cover similar terrain, the southern Nevada desert.

SCORE's annual spring event is the Great Mojave 250, held in and around the small town of Lucerne, California. This race consists of three laps of about 80 miles (128 kilometers) each over rough desert terrain. Part of its challenge lies in the fact that the course becomes more and more chewed up each time around, and nothing is predictable.

The SCORE Baja Internacional, often referred to as the Baja 500, takes place in early June. Half as long as the Baja 1000, it's still a grueling race that covers many different kinds of terrain around Ensenada, where it begins and ends.

Off-road racers celebrate the Fourth of July with fireworks of a different sort: the HDRA Fireworks 250 at Barstow, California. And in September, competitors travel to Craig, Colorado, for the HDRA Colorado 300.

The few hardy competitors who finish all eight of these races in a year are honored by membership in the Toyota Milestone Club. Those who have completed six out of the eight races (three SCORE and three HDRA) are eligible for the Toyota True Grit Award, given to the competitor whose average miles per hour is the fastest. Like the class championships, this award carries a monetary reward, and competitors can win up to $10,000.

PRE-RUNNING

Even if it is their first off-road race, most drivers will have already pre-run, or driven the course, at least once. During this run, they take note of hazards and think about how they will drive the course during the race. Where will they try to make fast time, and where will they slow down to avoid getting stuck? Most competitors write all this information on a map of the route.

Rather than pre-run the course in their racing vehicles, drivers use "pre-runners" — trucks that are rugged enough to cover the terrain. Although these trucks aren't geared for racing, they are equipped with special front and back bumpers, suspension systems, and other extra equipment.

Many competitors are still working on their racing vehicles up to the day before their arrival in Ensenada. Yet even these people take time out to pre-run, knowing it will save them time in the end and could possibly mean the difference between victory and defeat.

THE FUTURE

You don't have to live in California or the southwestern United States to see or participate in off-road races. This sport is becoming more popular

Getting ready for another race.

every year. In certain climates, races are scheduled only during the months when the weather is likely to cooperate. Northern states can be the scene of some exciting off-road events.

Enough people have become interested in off-road racing that there are now magazines devoted to the sport, and some races are routinely covered by sports channels on cable TV.

Off-road *riding* — getting off the beaten path and into the mountains, across the plains, or onto the beach — is an outdoor sport that the whole family can enjoy. Off-road *racing* is only for the very adventurous!

Class 2: Unlimited Two-Seater.

BAJA CAR DIVISIONS

The Buggy Division includes all four-wheel non-production and Volkswagen classes.

Class 1: Unlimited Single-Seaters. Here unlimited means unlimited power — any kind of engine. The vehicle must be a single-seater. The vehicles in this

41

Class 5: Unlimited Baja Bug.

category are usually specially-built dune buggies. Mark McMillin, the 1986 winner in this class (who also had the fastest time of all the cars in the 1986 Baja 1000), drives a car designed by the Chenowth company with a Porsche 6-cylinder engine.

Class 2: Unlimited Two-Seaters. Again, mostly dune buggies with unlimited power, these cars seat two people. Most of the buggies driven in this class are designed by such companies as Chenowth, Funco, and Raceco.

Class 1-1600 and 2-1600. The cars in this class are

Class 11: Showroom Stock Volkswagon Sedan.

identical to those in Class 1 or Class 2 except that they are restricted to 1600-cc engines.

Class 5: Unlimited Baja Bug. These are modified Volkswagen Beetles with unlimited engine power.

Class 5-1600. The Baja Bug with a 1600-cc VW engine.

Class 10: Single or Two-Seat Dune Buggies with 1650-cc Engine. The bodies of the cars in Classes 9 and 10 have been modified, but they all have VW 1650-cc engines produced by various manufacturers.

Class 11: Showroom Stock Volkswagen Sedans. These are basic VW Beetles with bodies intact.

Challenger Class. This class is for first-time competitors in any of the buggy classes.

The Heavy Metal Division includes full-sized production sedans, pickup trucks, and four-wheel-drive vehicles.

Class 3: 4x4 Short Wheelbase. Production four-wheel-drive vehicles with a short wheelbase include such vehicles as the Jeep CJ-7, Jeep Cherokee, Dodge Ramcharger, and Ford Bronco.

Class 4: 4x4 Long Wheelbase. Production four-wheel-drive vehicles with a long wheelbase include veteran Class 4 winner Rod Hall's Dodge pickups as well as the Jeep J-10.

Class 6: Two-Wheel-Drive Sedans. This class is for normal passenger cars, and recent winning cars include a 1955 Chevrolet, a 1968 Saab, and a 1965 Ford Ranchero.

Class 8: Two-Wheel-Drive Heavyweight Pickups. This class contains Fords, Dodges, and other full-size pickup trucks.

Class 14: 4x4 Unlimited. In this class, any vehicle qualifies as long as it has four-wheel drive.

The Mini Metal Division is for mini and mid-sized production pickup trucks and four-wheel-drive vehicles.

Class 8: Two-Wheel-Drive Heavyweight Pickup.

Class 7: Mini or Mid-Sized Pickups. The Chevy S-10, Ford Ranger, Nissan, Toyota, and Mazda represent some of the recent winners in this class.

Class 7S: Stock Mini or Mid-Sized Pickups. The trucks in this category are the same kind driven in Class 7, with one difference: these are showroom stock, driven as delivered rather than modified or specially outfitted by their owners.

Class 7 4x4: Mini or Mid-Sized Pickups with Four-Wheel Drive.

FOR MORE INFORMATION

For more information on Baja cars and Baja races, write to:
SCORE International
31356 Via Colinas, Suite 111
Westlake Village, CA 91362

High Desert Racing Association
12997 Las Vegas Boulevard
Las Vegas, NV 89124

GLOSSARY/INDEX

ALL-TERRAIN VEHICLE (ATV) 6 — *A three-wheel vehicle, similar to a motorcycle, designed to be driven on all kinds of terrain either for recreation or in competition.*

CHASE CREW TRUCK 24, 25 — *This vehicle, equipped with spare parts, tools, and even mechanics, follows the race car's route on ordinary roads and is ready to help the racing vehicle in an emergency.*

CHASSIS 16 — *The frame of a car.*

FOUR-WHEEL DRIVE 5, 6, 44, 45 — *In a vehicle with four-wheel drive, all four wheels of a vehicle receive power from the engine; in two-wheel-drive vehicles, only two wheels (the front or the rear) receive power. The axle for the other two wheels is "dead" and the wheels turn only when pushed by the wheels on the "live" axle.*

ODYSSEY 6 — *A type of all-terrain vehicle that is not much bigger than the three-wheel ATVs. Odyssey racers are equipped with steering wheels, wide tires, and powerful engines.*

PRE-RUNNING 39 — *Driving the race route in advance to discover the obstacles and determine how to avoid them. Trucks used for this purpose are called pre-runners.*

QUAD 6 — *An ATV with four wheels. A quad differs from a car in the kind of frame and engine it has.*

GLOSSARY/INDEX

ROLL BAR 20 — *A bar bolted or welded behind the driver's seat or in the truck bed to protect anyone inside if the vehicle flips over. The roll bar is an add-on item.*

ROLL CAGE 20 — *A cage completely surrounding the driver. The roll cage is part of the chassis of a vehicle.*

STOCK 44, 45 — *In the same condition as sold at the dealer or delivered from the factory, not modified. Stone stock means "absolutely stock."*

SUSPENSION 16, 17, 26, 39 — *The components, consisting of springs, stabilizer and torsion bars, control arms, strut rods, ball joints, and other parts, that connect a vehicle's chassis to the axles.*

WHEELBASE 44 — *The distance between the front and rear tires of a car.*